# Needle Tatting Necklace Guide Book

*With Step by Step Instructions and Crochet Patterns*

Steven N Egbert

# Table of Contents

| | |
|---|---:|
| CHAPTER ONE | 5 |
| CHAPTER TWO | 10 |
| CHAPTER THREE | 13 |
| CHAPTER FOUR | 18 |
| CHAPTER FIVE | 28 |

## COPYRIGHT PAGE

All rights reserved. No part of this publication may be reproduced in any form or means without prior written permission to the copy right holder.

Copyright (c) 2023

INTRODUCTION

CHAPTER ONE

THE DIY OF TATTING NECKLACE (1 / 15 STEPS)

THE DIY OF TATTING NECKLACE (2 / 15 STEPS)

THE DIY OF TATTING NECKLACE (3 / 15 STEPS)

CHAPTER TWO

THE DIY OF TATTING NECKLACE (4 / 15 STEPS)

THE DIY OF TATTING NECKLACE (5 / 15 STEPS)

THE DIY OF TATTING NECKLACE (6 / 15 STEPS)

CHAPTER THREE

THE DIY OF TATTING NECKLACE (7 / 15 STEPS)

THE DIY OF TATTING NECKLACE (8 / 15 STEPS)

THE DIY OF TATTING NECKLACE (9 / 15 STEPS)

CHAPTER FOUR

THE DIY OF TATTING NECKLACE (10 / 15 STEPS)

THE DIY OF TATTING NECKLACE (11 / 15 STEPS)

THE DIY OF TATTING NECKLACE (12 / 15 STEPS)

CHAPTER FIVE

THE DIY OF TATTING NECKLACE (13 / 15 STEPS)

THE DIY OF TATTING NECKLACE (14 / 15 STEPS)

THE DIY OF TATTING NECKLACE (15 / 15 STEPS)

**INTRODUCTION**

Finally, after many tries and unsuccessful attempts, after many hours looking for a solution to make the necklace, I managed to decipher how to create it.

This is an opportunity to be immersed in artisans or training centers for crafts. Needle tatting technique is more recent. But be careful to choose special tatting needles to be sure you have the right equipment for this technique. For example, a mattress needle is not suitable for tatting: its eye is too big to form knots and its tip is too sharp to handle it easily.

# CHAPTER ONE

# THE DIY OF TATTING NECKLACE (1 / 15 STEPS)

## Step 1: Needle beads & adding beads

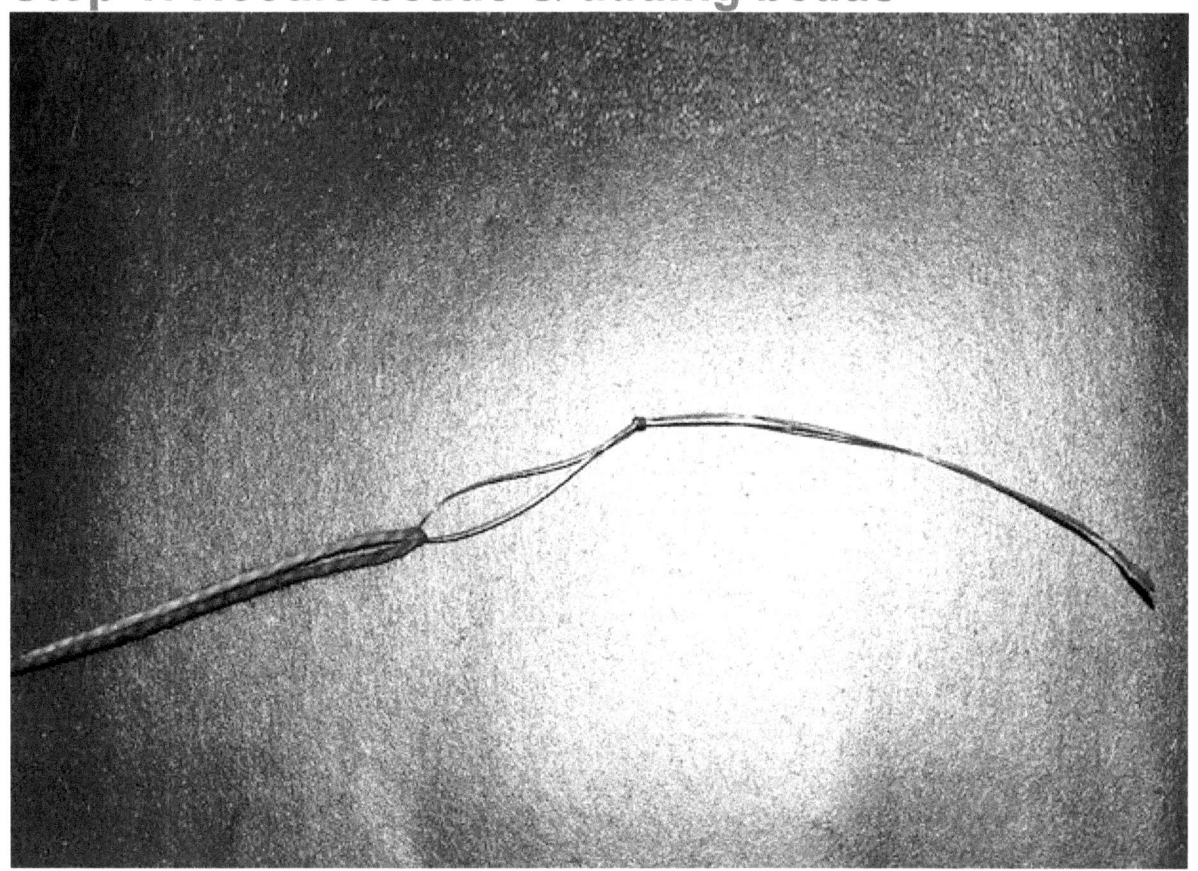

**This first step is very important!**

Before starting the work, we must introduce all the beads in the thread that are going to be needed for our work. The beads remain in the ball thread, waiting to be used when needed.

**Remark**:

If we are unsure of the exact total amount of beads we need to work on, you should be sure and make several more beads. It is better for us on pearls that we are not missing.

To enter the beads into the thread, I use several hours in search of a needle that will suffice appropriate, but none of the people I have had in my house have gone well. So I decided to create my own beading needle.

It's very simple: We take a piece of thin nylon peach thread, between 7 and 10 cm long, fold it in half and make a knot with the two ropes by half the length. Then gently and with the help of a lighter, heat the ends of the two to melt the nylon strings and press between your fingers to unite them. Ideally we would be like you see in the picture.

# THE DIY OF TATTING NECKLACE (2 / 15 STEPS)

## Step 2: prepare working materials

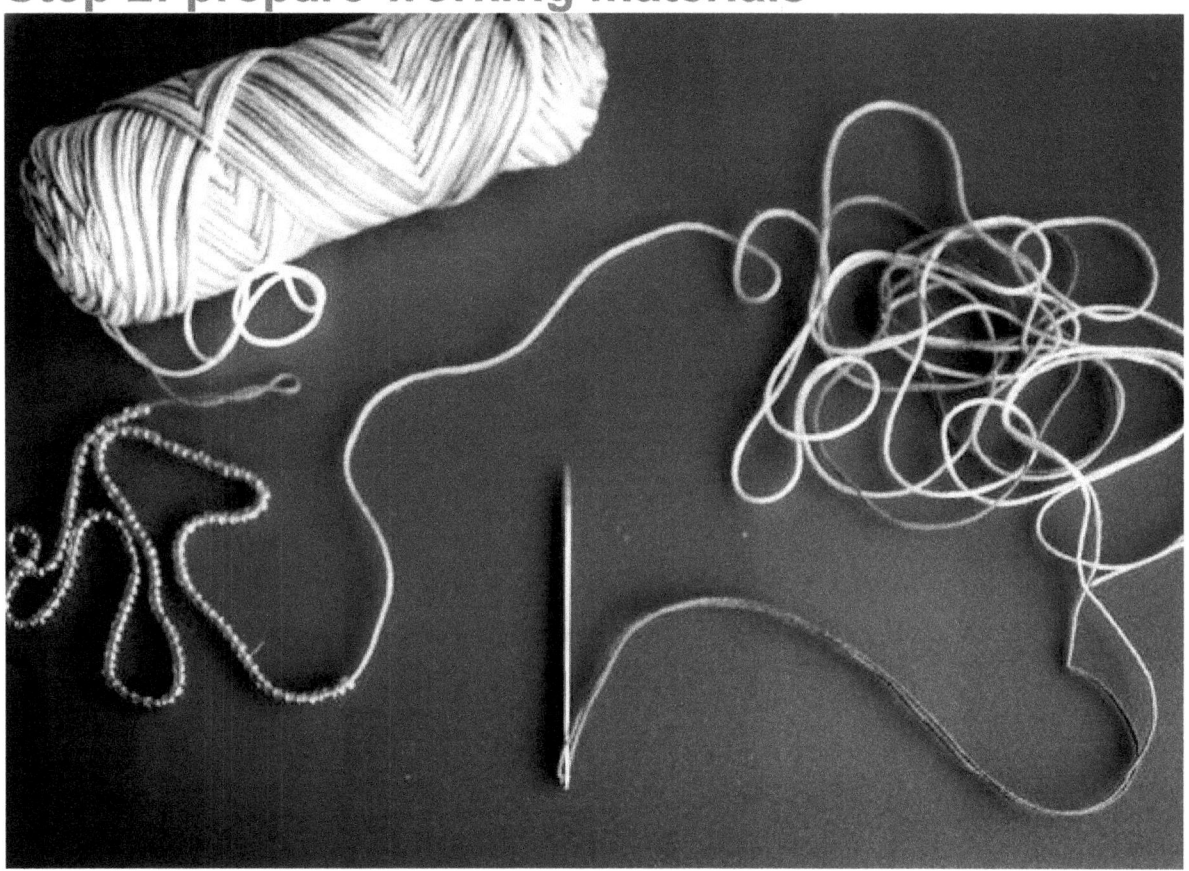

Once you have entered all the beads necessary to work in the thread, pass the thread through the hole of the tatting needle, and we will obtain a color desk that contrasts with the work, to give us a good job.

We have the yarn in the balloon, along with the beads, we are going to use for our work. In the needle we have the thread that we need to pass through inside the stitches of all the works. The thread is the same, but we will start in the middle of the thread, leaving on the right, the needle, all the long thread necessary to assemble the structure of the part. For this reason, we must leave quite a long thread in the needle.

Materials needed:

1 ball of cotton yarn (45 gr)

1 needle beads (I explain how to do it in the previous step)

1 tatting needle (size according to your yarn size)

1 crochet hook (size according to your wire size)

100 crystal beads approximately (not recommended plastic beads, because if you need iron for work they can be wrong)

**Remark:**

Try to choose a range of colors for yarn and counts, to coordinate properly.

## THE DIY OF TATTING NECKLACE (3 / 15 STEPS)

### Step 3: achieve the double point: first semester

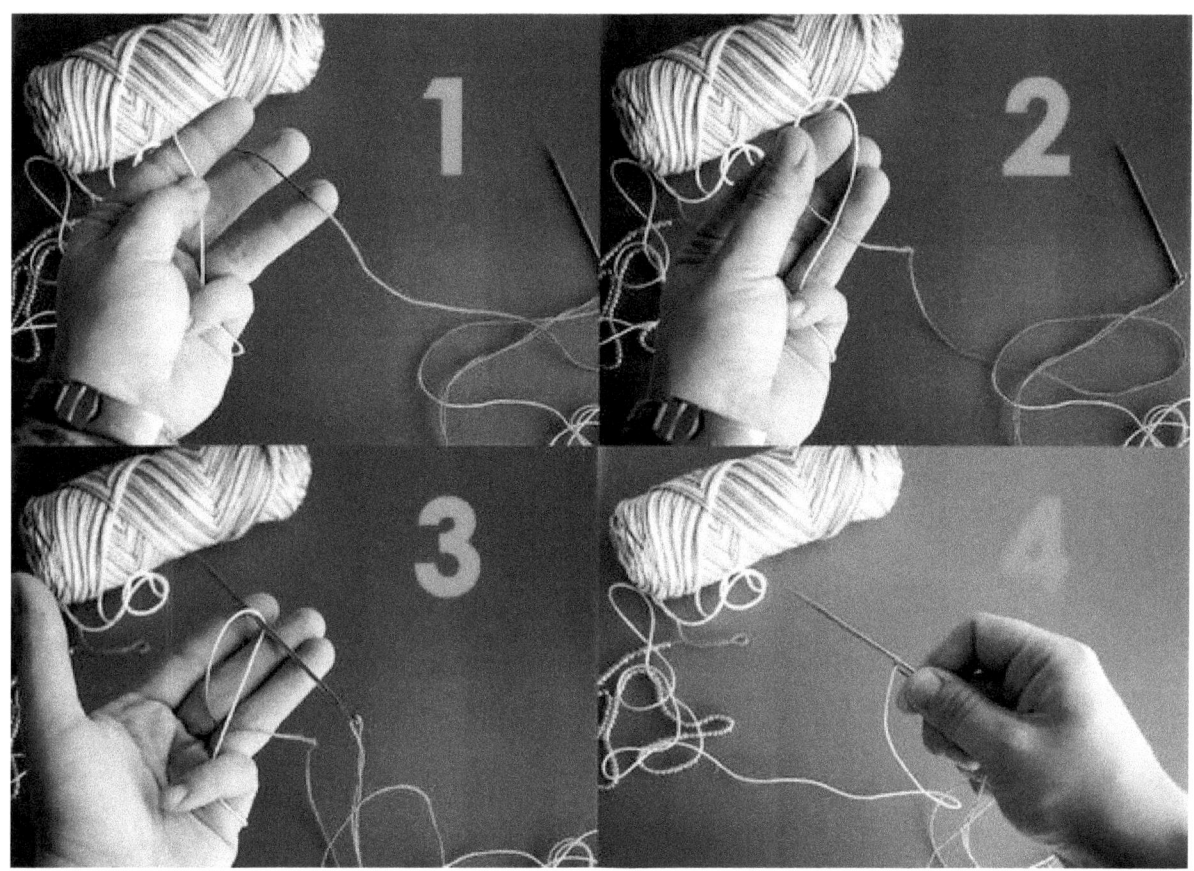

The Double Point

Is the basic point for tatting. It consists of two halves, which are two knots around the needle, the right and the backhand suite, as you can see in this and the next step of the Instruction.

First half of the point

Yarn in left hand is ball. Insert needle as shown, then remove finger and pull yarn tight to put stitch on needle.

# CHAPTER TWO

# THE DIY OF TATTING NECKLACE (4 / 15 STEPS)

## Step 4: make the double stitch: second half

**Second half of the point**

Insert needle as shown, then remove finger and pull yarn tight to put stitch on needle.

**Remark:**

It is very important to tighten the stitches, so that the work will be neat and compact, then the stitches, we were not open or stretched more than they should.

Likewise, it is also important to choose the appropriate size of the needle for each thickness of the yarn that we will be using. The needle should never be thicker than the thread of our work.

# THE DIY OF TATTING NECKLACE (5 / 15 STEPS)

## Step 5: make a picot

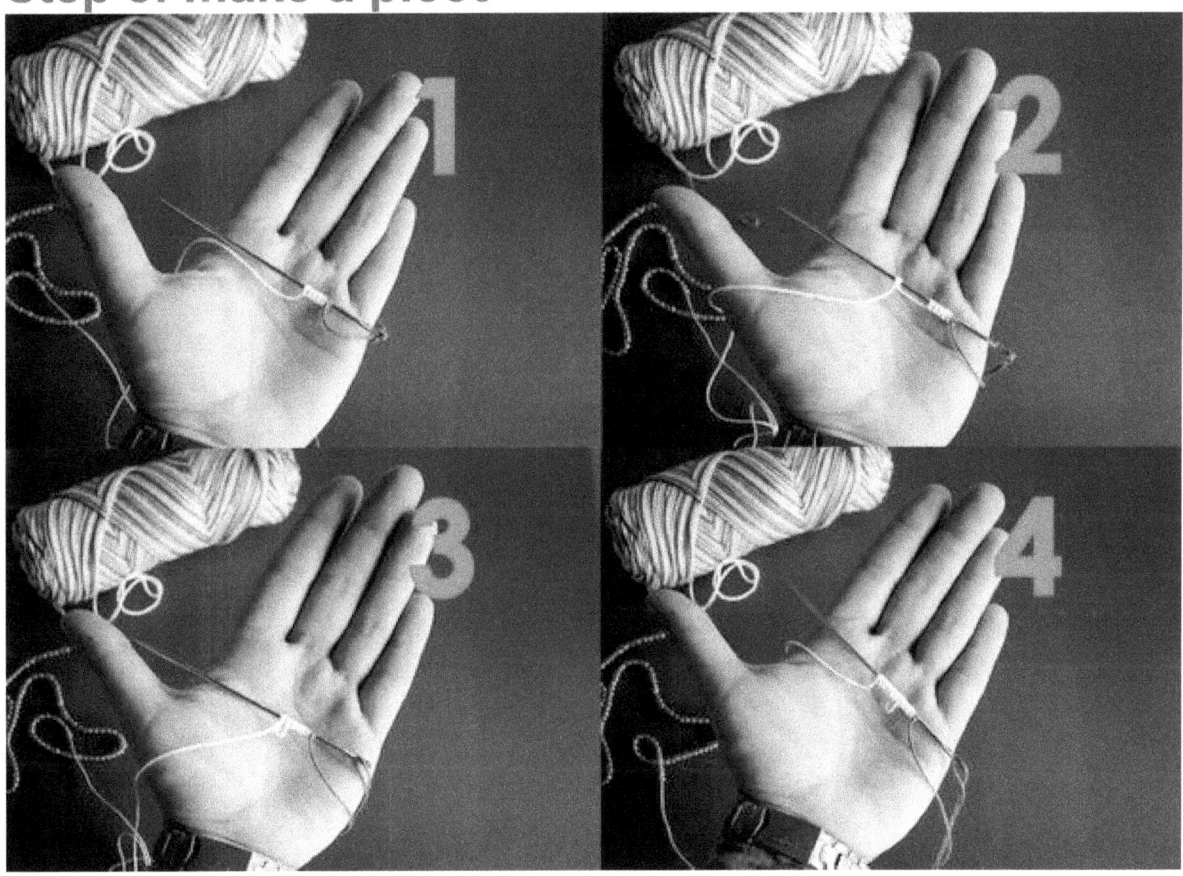

**Picot prick (abbrevation. p)**

Finish the first half of the stitch as before, but use your right hand finger to keep a space between the stitches already on the needle and the first half of the stitch.

**Remark:**

The pins are used to join the different shapes and works and are also decorative elements of the piece.

For this reason, when Picot joins pieces, we make it shorter, but since then, going through the Picot yarn and stretching, we also could enlarge the hole and leave the dirty work and poor finish. On the other hand, when Picot serves as decoration, we will do it as long as we want them or dictate the design pattern we do.

# THE DIY OF TATTING NECKLACE (6 / 15 STEPS)

## Step 6: basic shapes: chains and rings

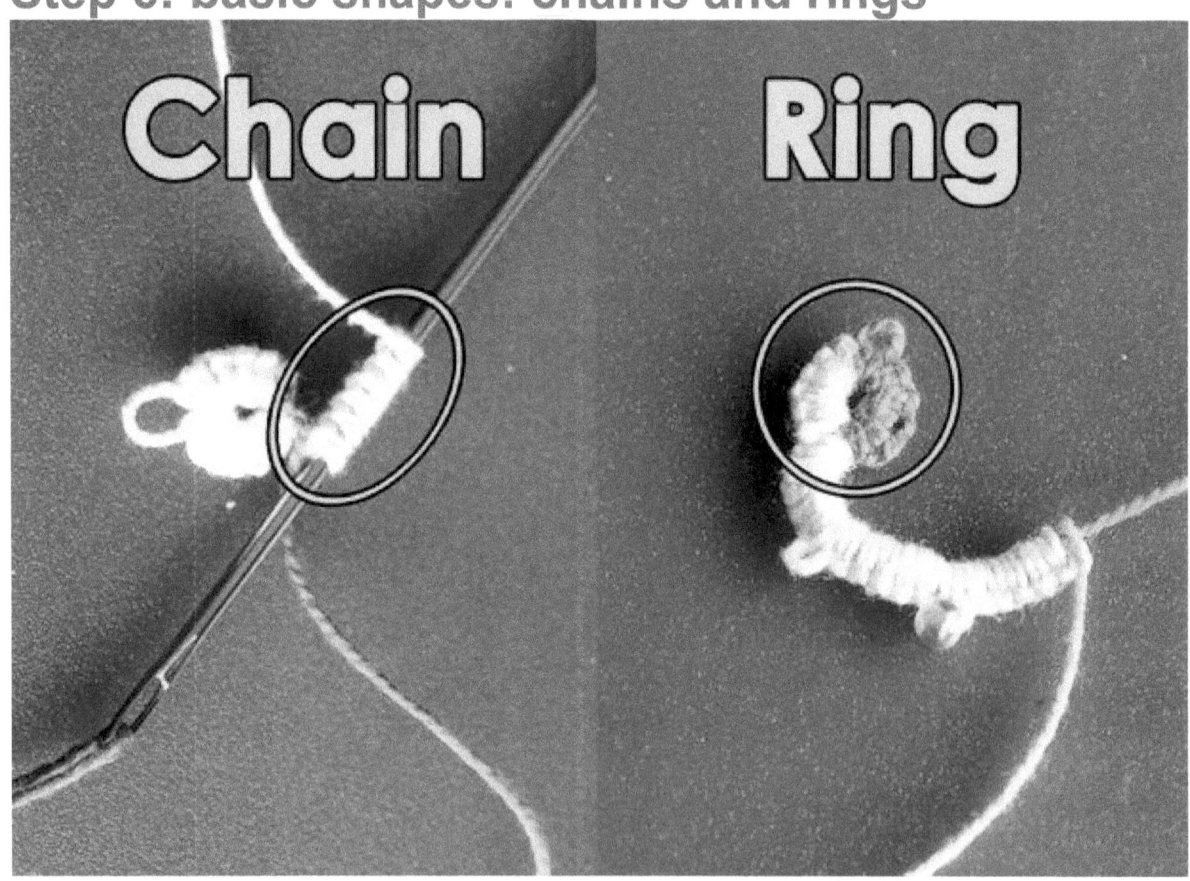

In the art of lace are 2 basic points, the Double point ( ds ) and the Picot point ( p ).

These are also the two basic methods for mounting these stitches, the chain ( Ch ) and the ring ( R ).

The chain is a series of stitches, through which the thread passes and is not closed.

The ring is a series of stitches, through which the thread passes, closing at the end to form the ring.

Chains and rings can be formed from different stitches in succession, alternating between Double stitch and Picot stitch.

If we can find patterns like these:

Ch-4p2p2p2p4-yo ( yo is spun, thanks to the inside of the dots)

R-6 p 6-Cl ( Cl is near the ring)

# CHAPTER THREE

## THE DIY OF TATTING NECKLACE (7 / 15 STEPS)

Step 7: make a ring

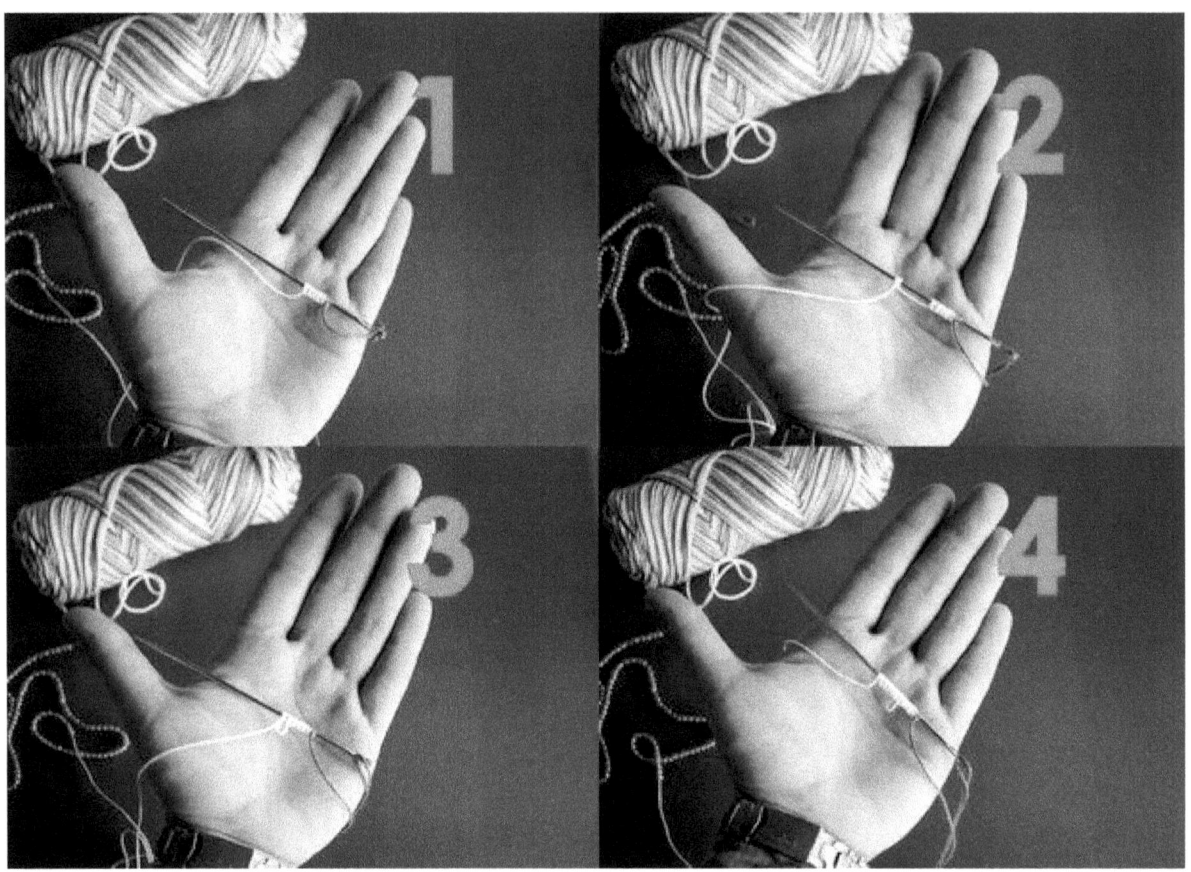

Ring (abbrevation R)

We are going to make our first ring!

First mount ds 6, we have 1 Picot and once again mount ds 6.

Then just close the ring, passing the thread of the needle through the stitches, but with his left hand holding the end of the thread where the work begins, forming a loop through which the needle passes to close the 'ring.

In a model we find well annotated: R-6 p 6-Cl

Remark:

If you look at the images displayed can see how to close the ring in detail.

# THE DIY OF TATTING NECKLACE (8 / 15 STEPS)

## Step 8: start the necklace!

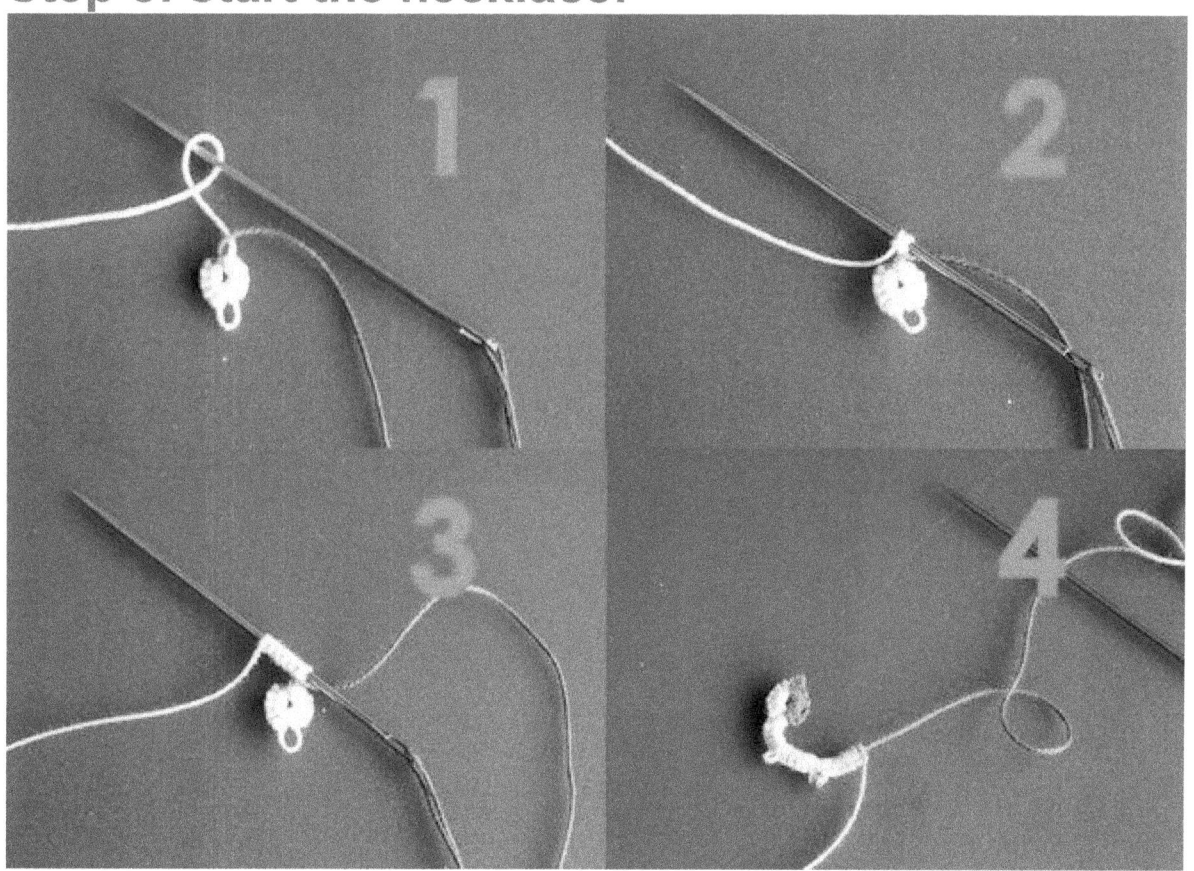

We will start the necklace following the pattern. Continue the pattern instructions:

1 - R-6 p 6-Cl-rw ( rw means turn)

2 - ch-6p6B6-yo-rw ( B means a bead, which will introduce to work in the same space as a Picot could do)

Notes:

To add a bead, you will only have to pick up the thread of the needle, and then we carry out the following stitches.

At each step of the instruction, adding shorthand notation that you have come home to the most familiar will go.

Also you have the support of photos and illustrations to explain how it should be the shape of the piece you are doing at every moment.

# THE DIY OF TATTING NECKLACE (9 / 15 STEPS)

## Step 9: second ring & second chain

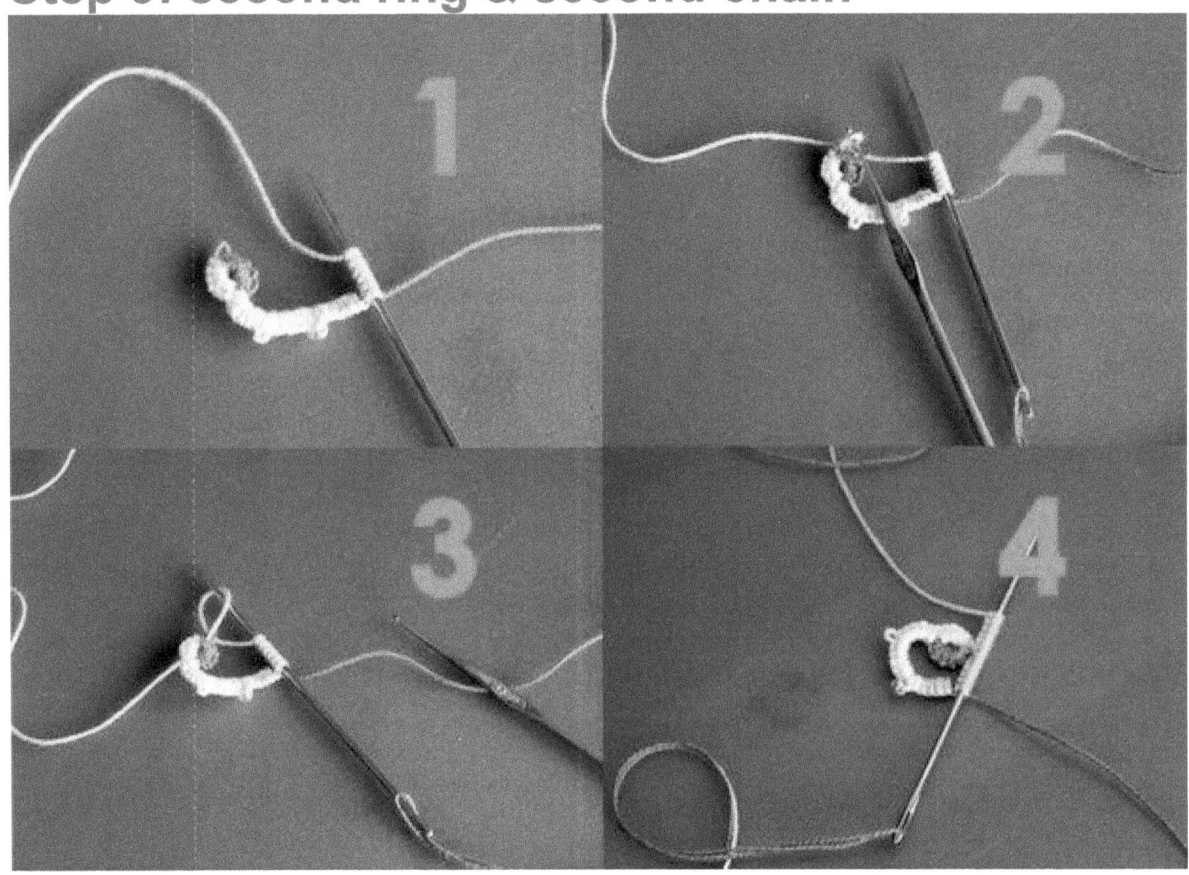

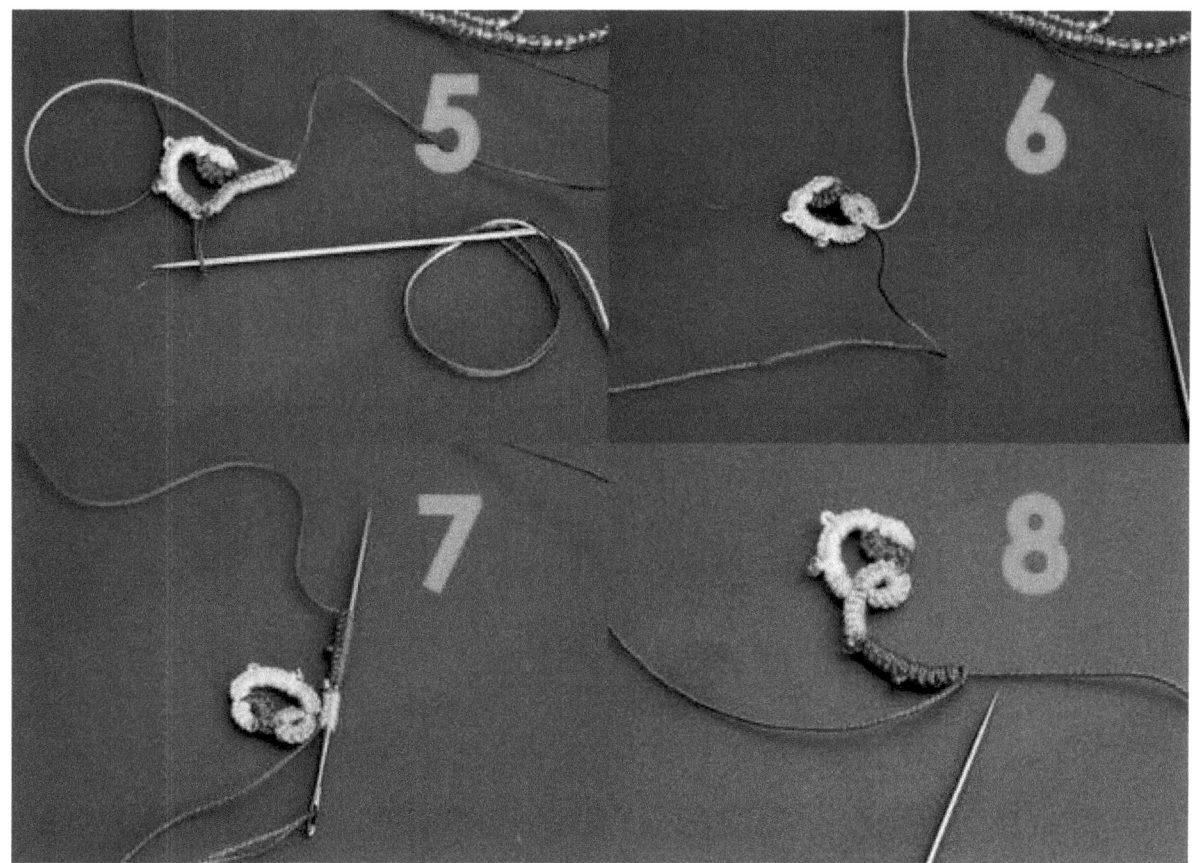

Work will continue to follow the pattern. We will make the second crown, first we put 6 ds on the needle and then replace the Picot, which connects the work on the Picot point of the first ring, therefore, with the help of a crochet needle, pass the yarn from the ball through the Picot stitch of the first ring and put the loop on the needle closer to yarn, then continue to add more 6 ds to the needle and finally close the second ring as usual.

We will continue to make the second chain (remember: we have to examine the work each time), this time add 6 ds first to the needle, then add a bead, plus 6 ds a Picot and 6 ds more and finally, pass the yarn through the needle stitches, to continue the work.

Continue the pattern instructions:

3 - R-6 + 6-Cl-rw

4 - ch-6B6p6-yo-rw

# CHAPTER FOUR

# THE DIY OF TATTING NECKLACE (10 / 15 STEPS)

## Step 10: next steps: the lower part of the necklace

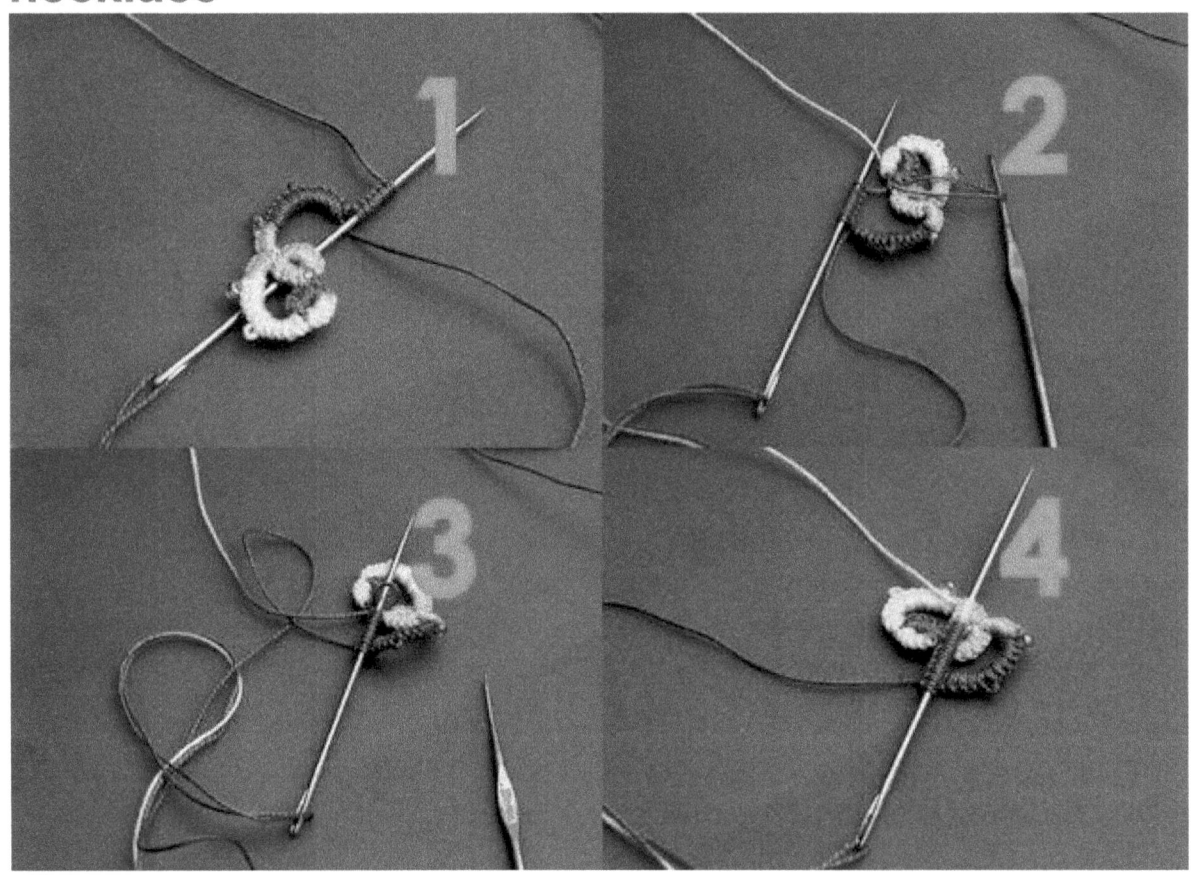

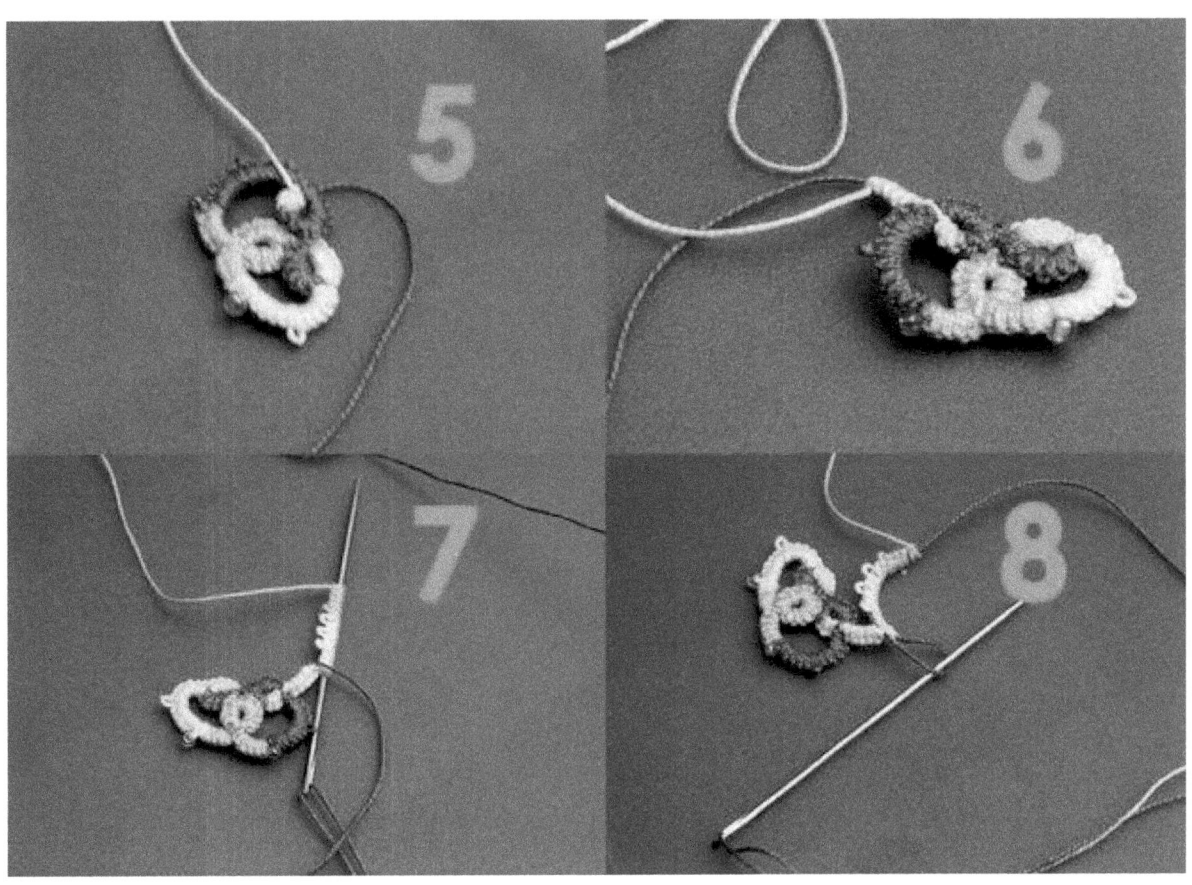

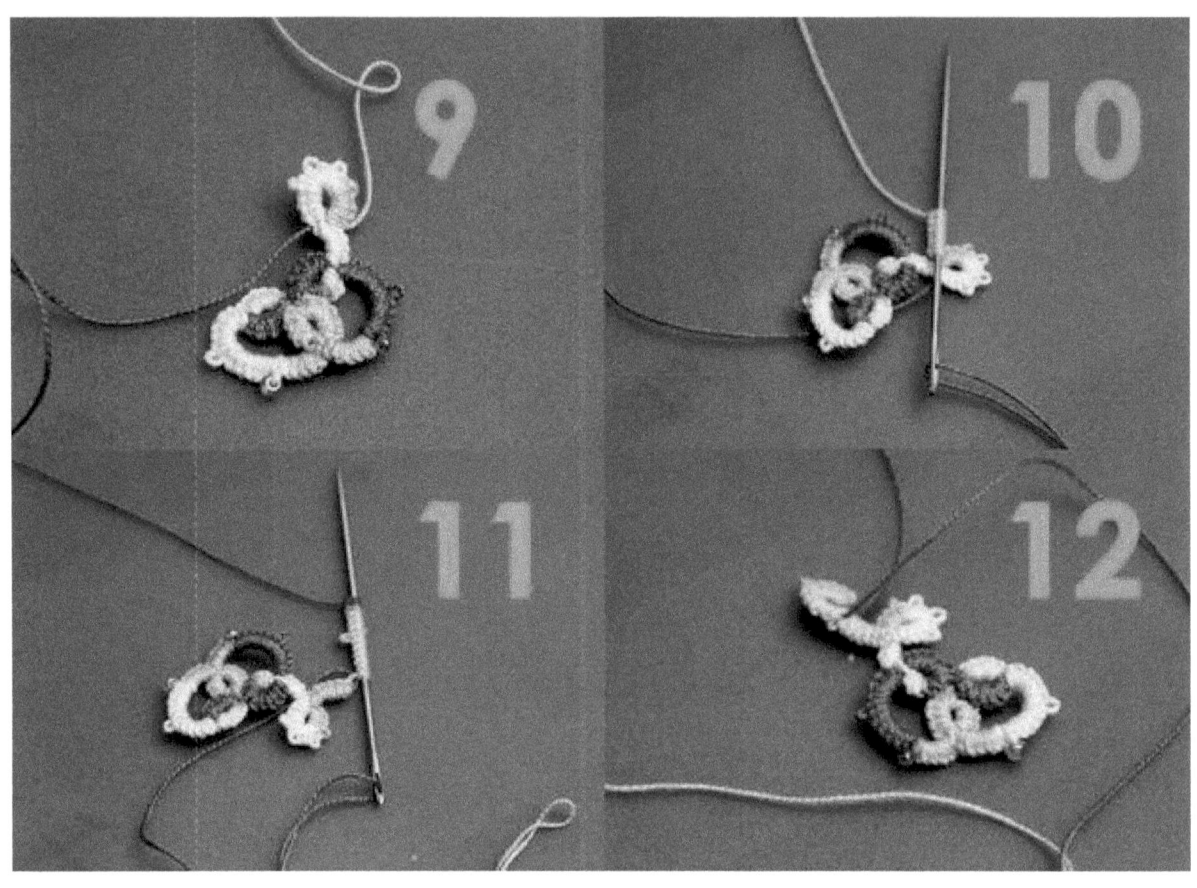

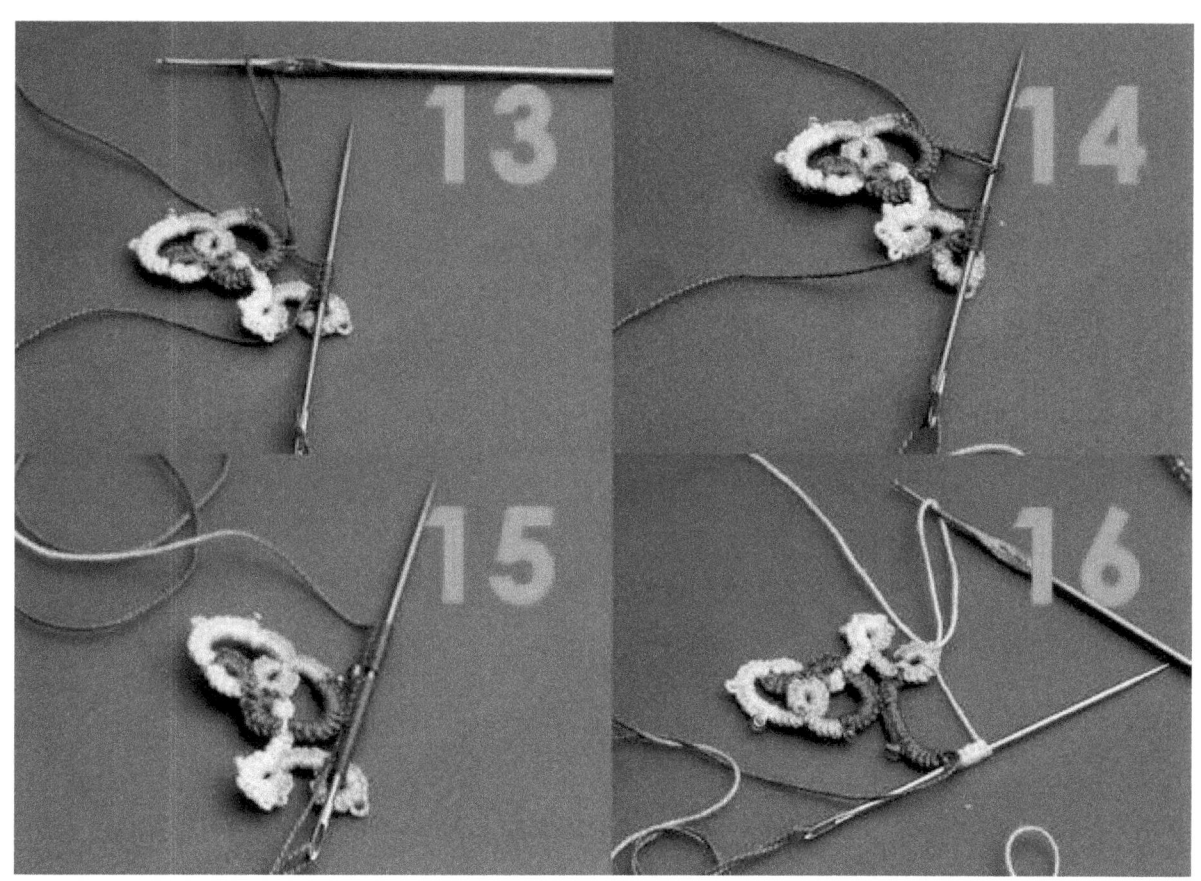

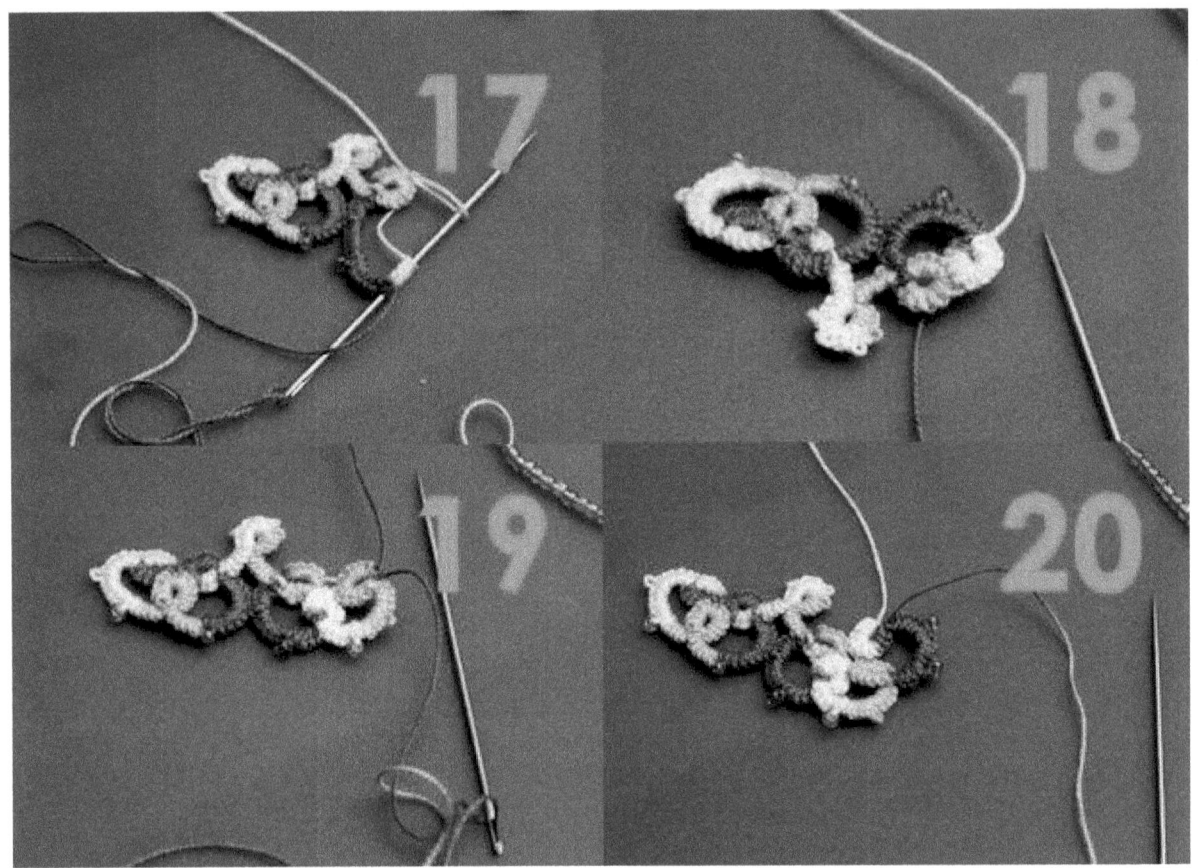

This part of the collar, is the bottom, which willdo go back to finish the job.

The necklace is finished in the middle, but we could change the pattern to finish at one end. For now we will start in this order and the assembly of the first part, which is very useful to go and check the performance the work done correctly all the necessary points and forms.

Continue the pattern instructions:

5 - R-6 + 6-Cl-rw

6 - ch-6-yo-rw

7 - R-4p2p2p2p4-Cl-rw

8 - ch-6-yo-rw

9 - R-6 p 6-Cl-rw

10 - ch-6 + 6 b 6-yo-rw (join the chain with the chain Picot stitch after)

11 - R-6 + 6-Cl-rw (join the ring with the first ring, which n not attached with the others of this part)

12 - ch-6B6p6-yo-rw

13 - R-6 + 6-Cl-rw

# THE DIY OF TATTING NECKLACE (11 / 15 STEPS)

## Step 11: next steps: the top of the necklace

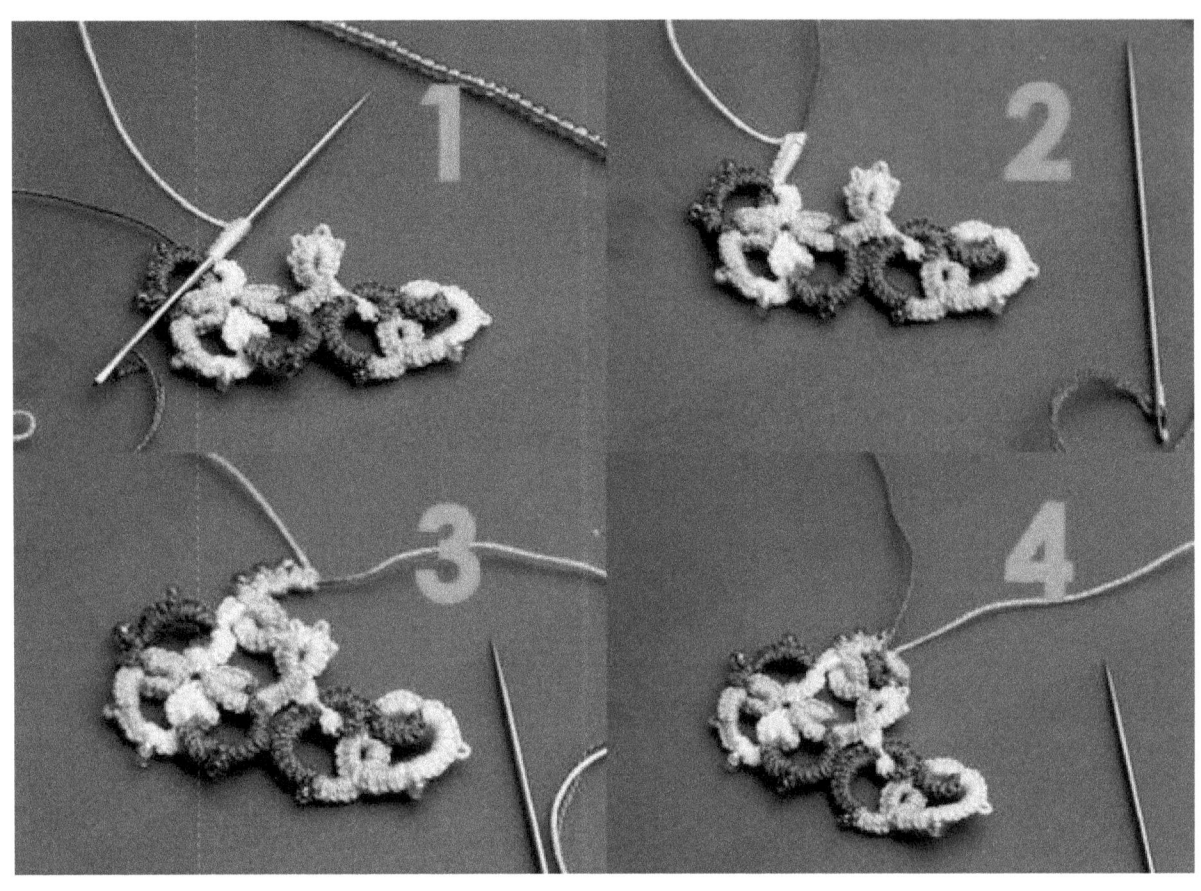

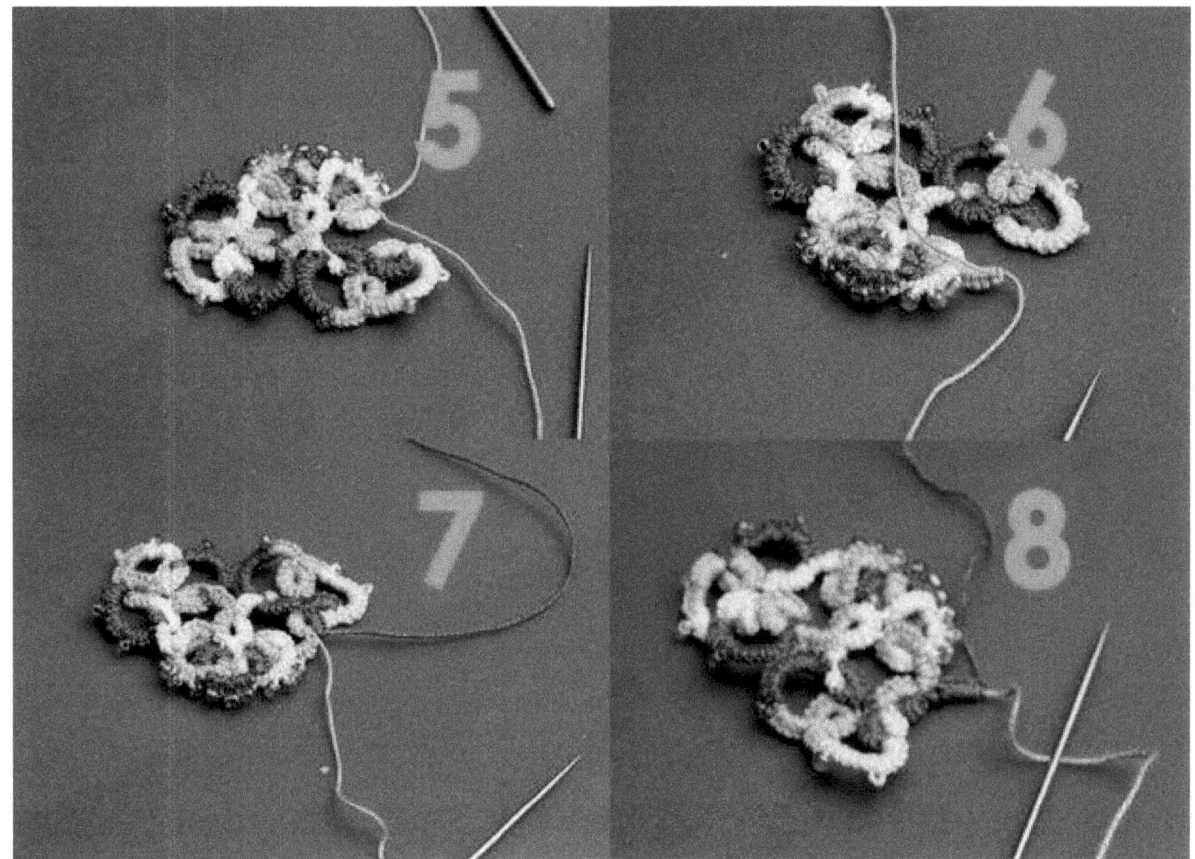

This part of the necklace is up to the top, which will start working, and which will determine the length of our necklace.

Remark :

We must bear in mind that, when tied down, represents a third of their original long. It is for this reason that we should measure the length of the first finished module, to calculate how many modules you need to fill our necklace to the desired length.

Continue the pattern instructions:

14 - ch-6-yo-rw

15 - R-6 + 6-Cl-rw (join yarn with first Picot stitch of large ring with 4 Picots)

16 - ch-2B2B2B2-yo-rw (Repeat 15 to 16 4 times, for any Picot stitch large ring) 17 - ch-6-yo-rw 18 - R-6 + 6-Cl-rw (join the thread with the 3 rings at the bottom part) 19 - ch-6-yo-rw

# THE DIY OF TATTING NECKLACE (12 / 15 STEPS)

## Step 12: make the top modules

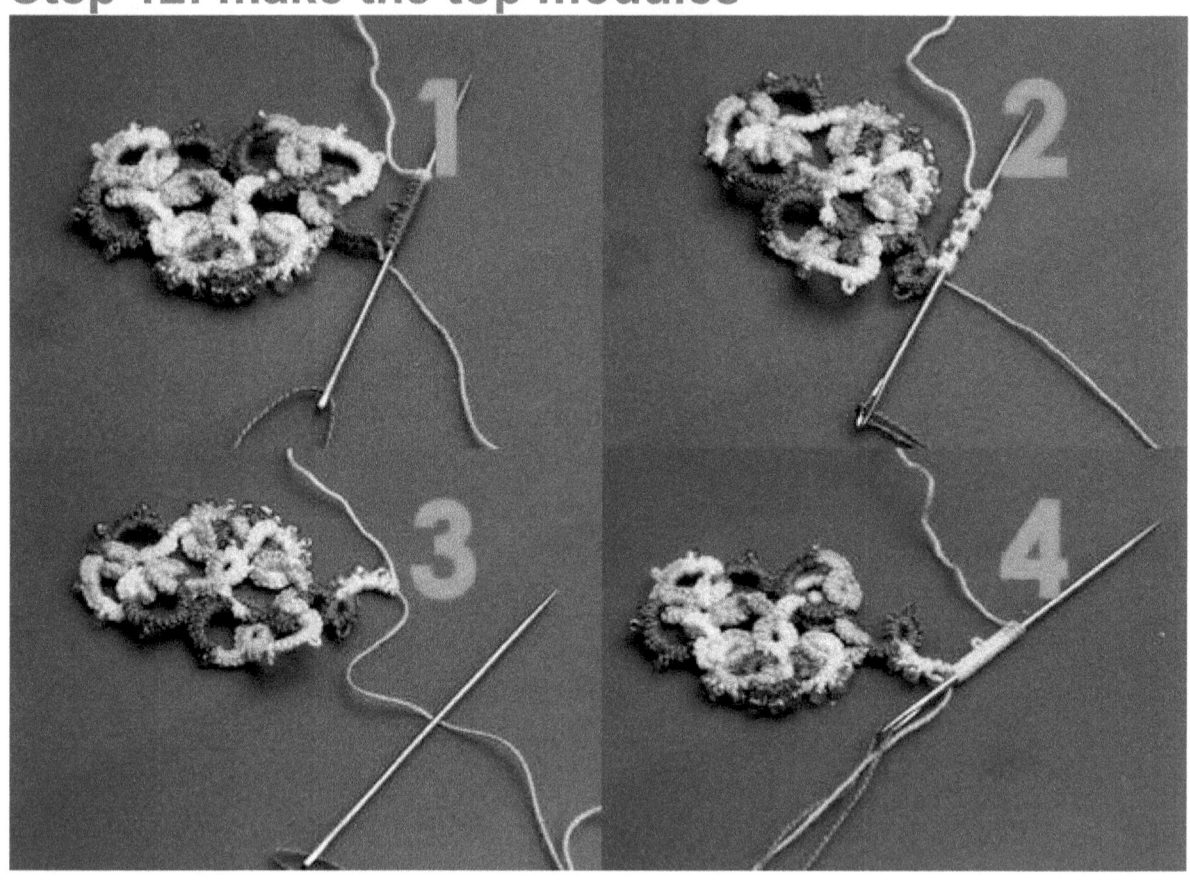

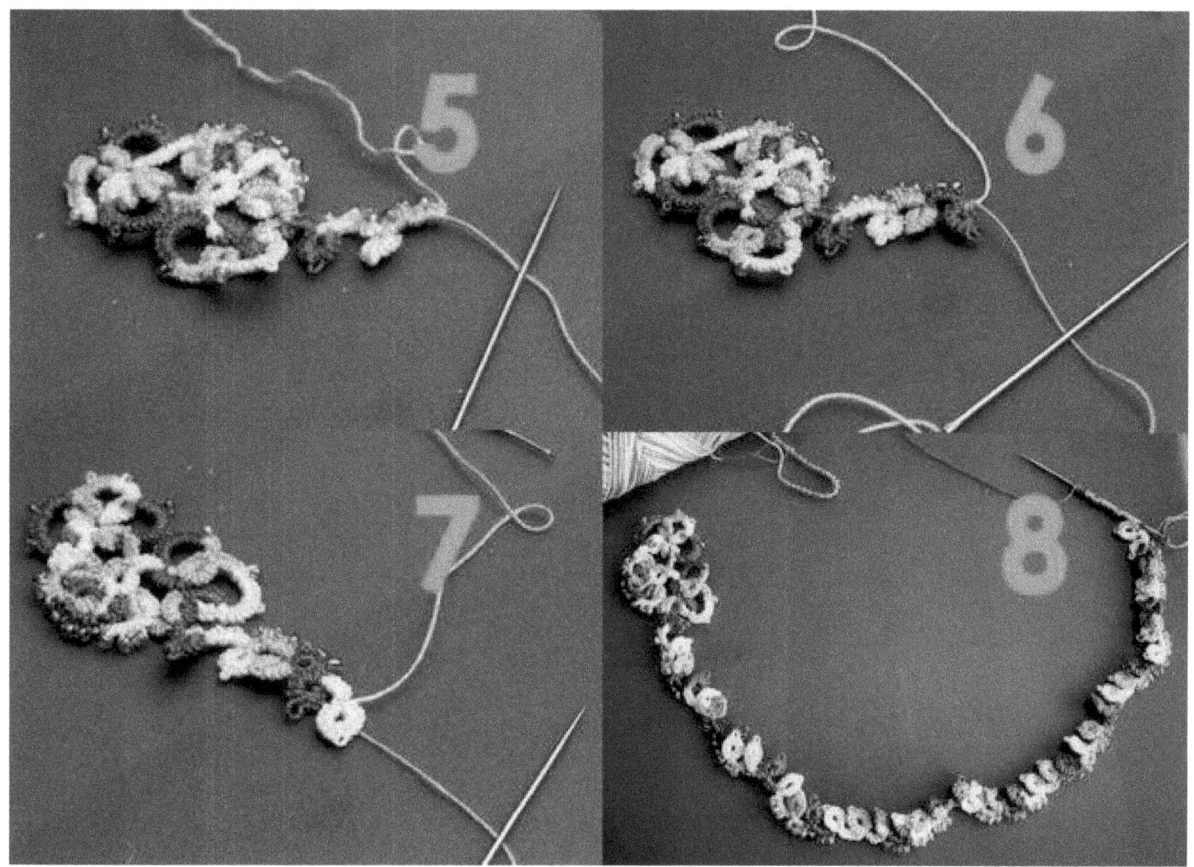

And at this time, when we have finished the first module of the collar, and we will start making the top of the collar, then close the work with the bottom.

From a chain with 6 ds.

Continue the pattern instructions:

19 - ch-6-yo-rw

20 - r-6 p 6-cl-rw

21 - ch-2b2b2b2-yo-rw (20 votes against 21, repeats it 4 times) 22 - ch-6-yo-rw 23 -r - 6p6-cl-rw

Repeat steps 19-23, which form the beginning of a module, as many times as necessary to reach the desired length for our necklace.

# CHAPTER FIVE

## THE DIY OF TATTING NECKLACE (13 / 15 STEPS)

### Step 13: next steps: the lower part of the necklace

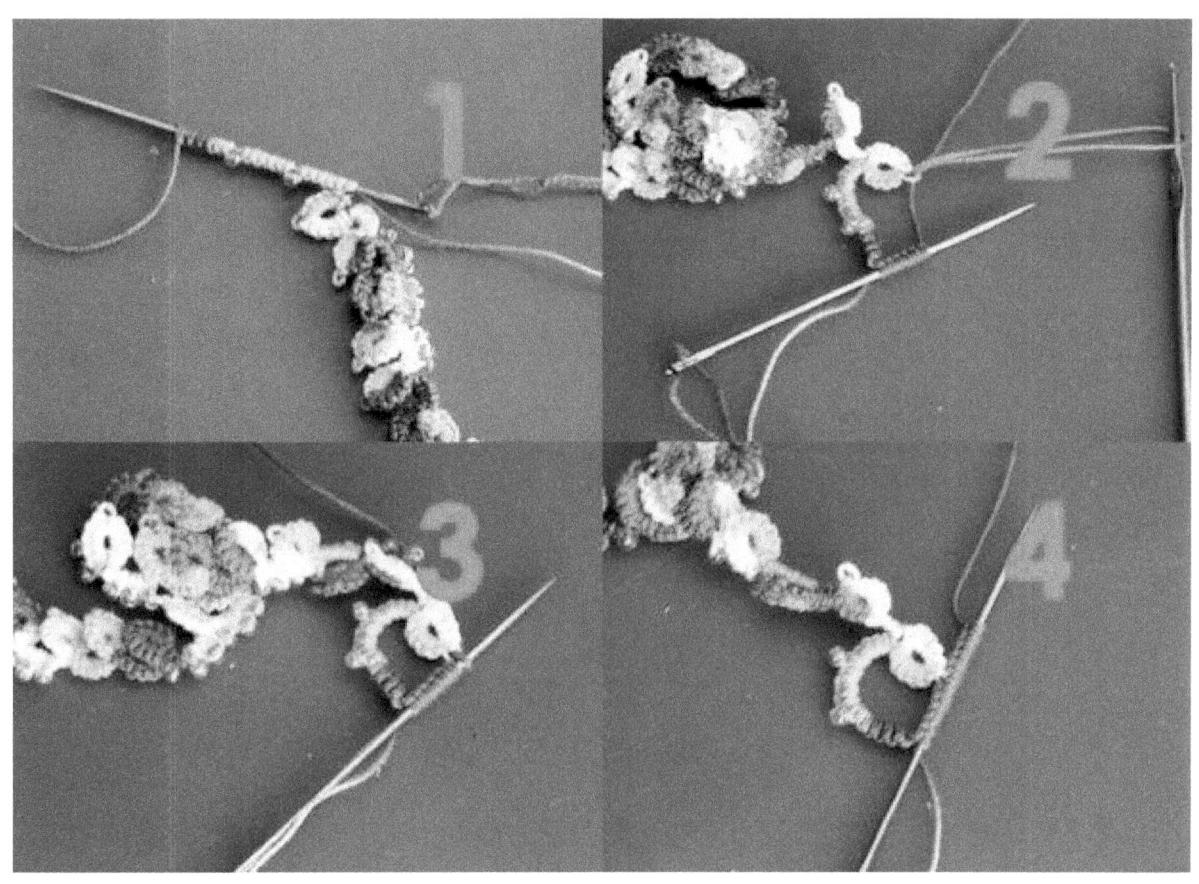

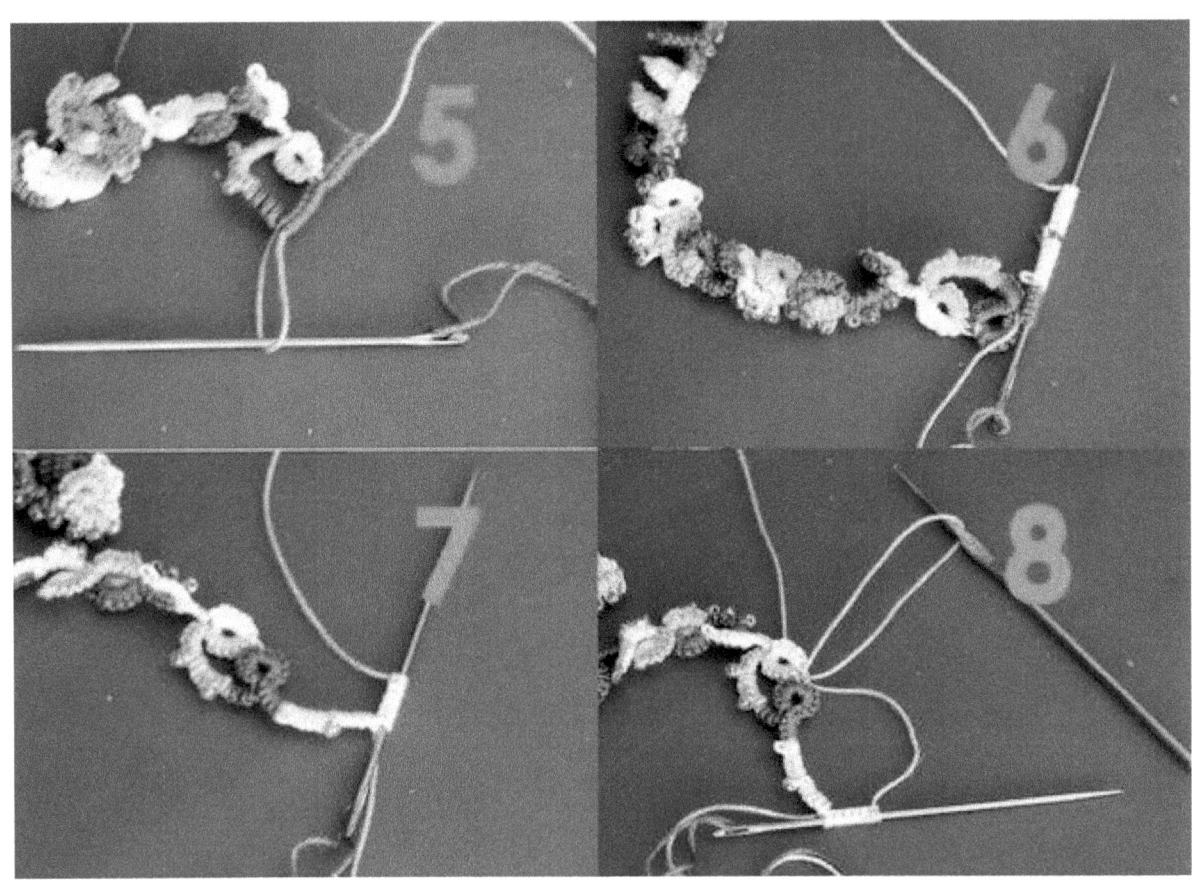

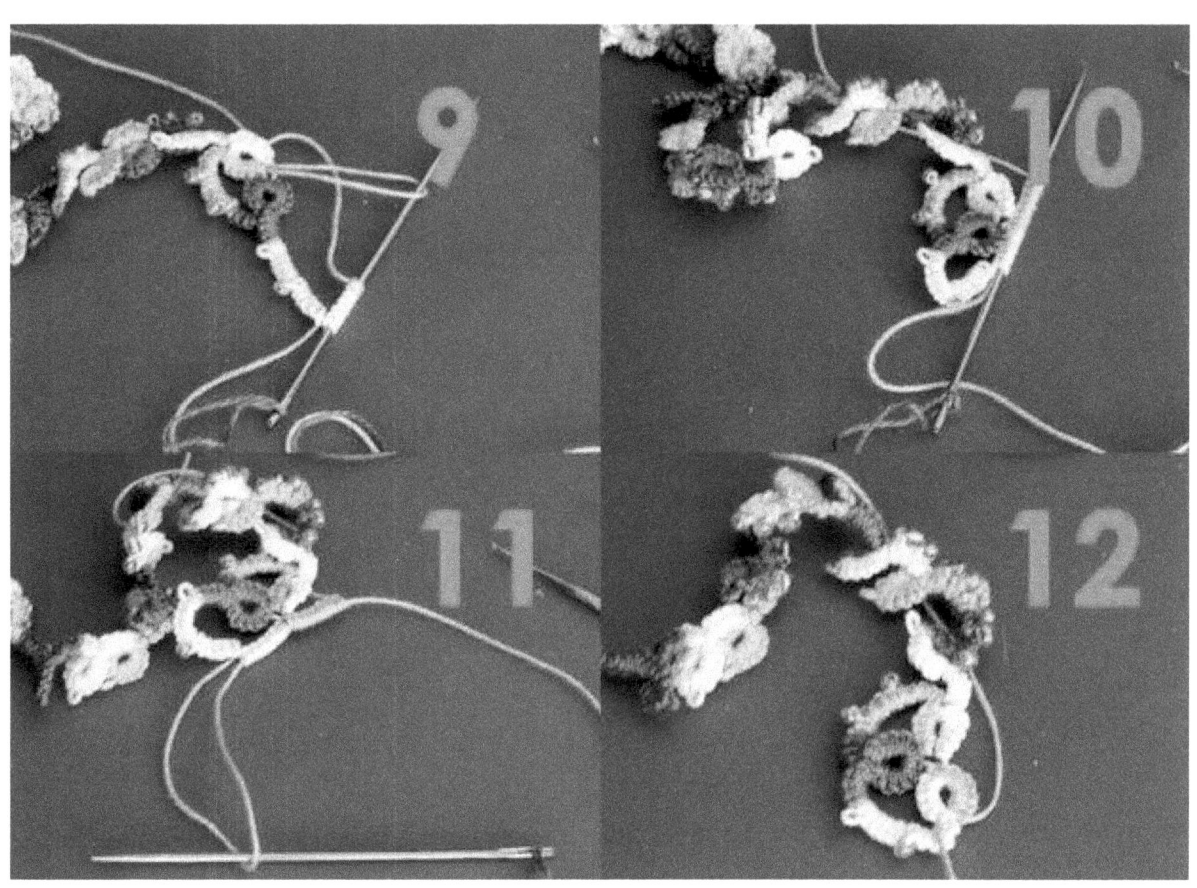

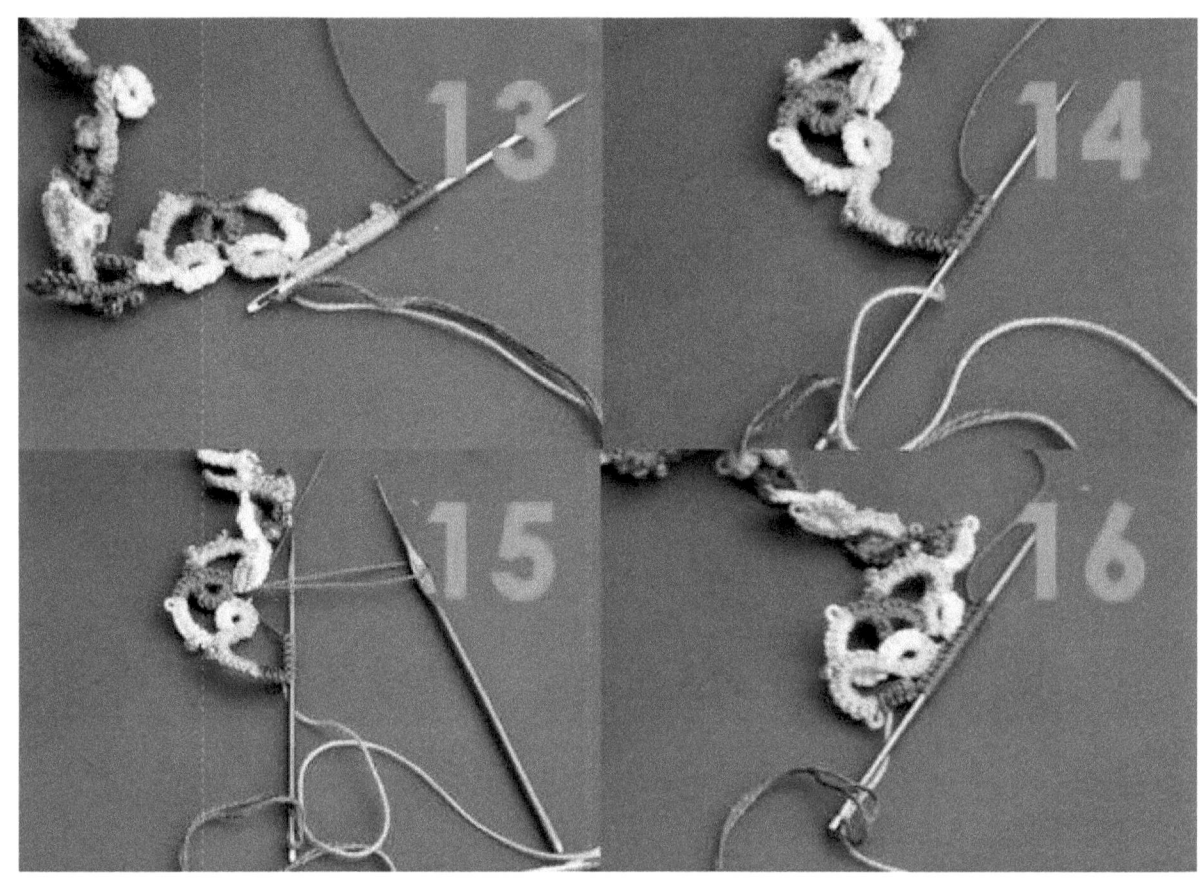

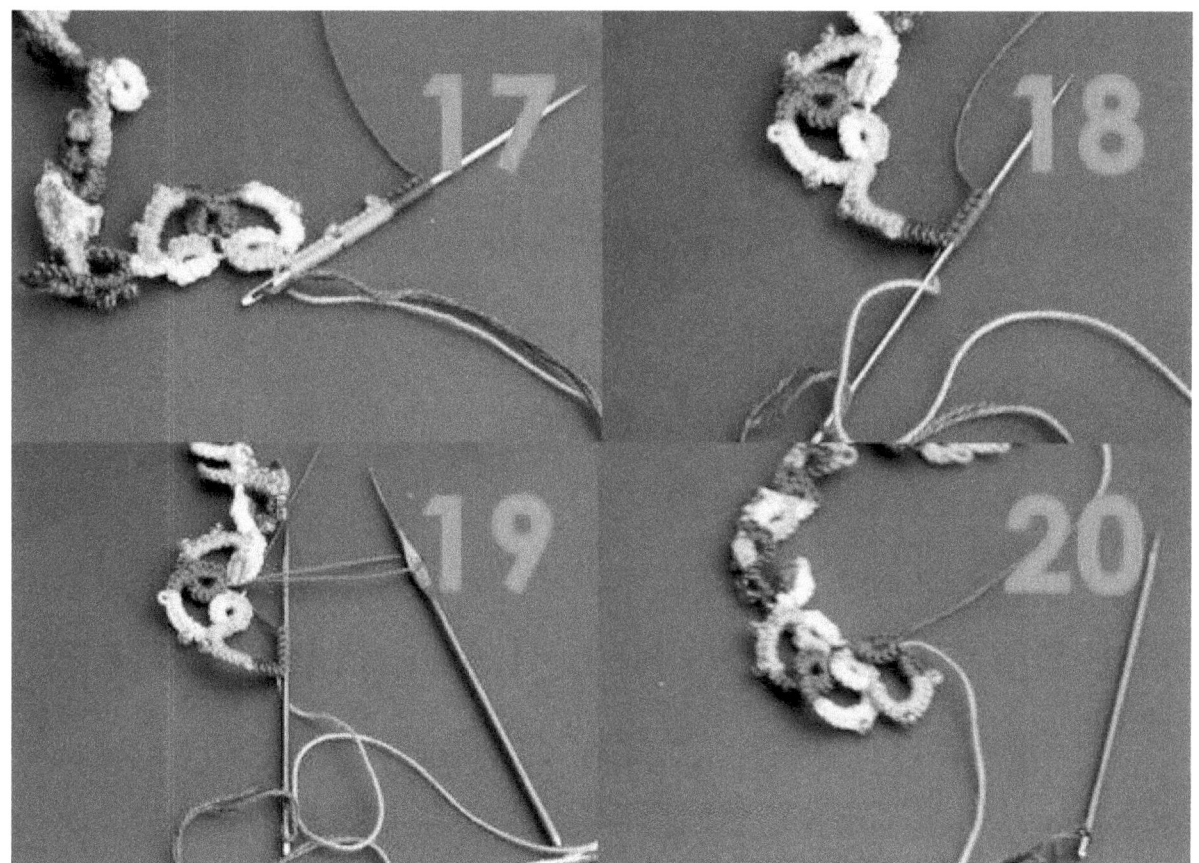

Once we have made the top of our necklace, let's start at the bottom, so that we can close the modules that look good and finish the necklace.

The upper part of the modules is made in step 23, regardless of the number of repeated modules as we need.

First of all, we will close this final module following the same model set up in the initial module.

We will continue with the model:

24 - ch-6B6p6-yp-rw

25 - R-6 + 6-Cl-rw

26 - ch-6p6B6-yo-rw

27 - R-6 + 6-Cl-rw

28 - ch-6B6p6-yo-rw

29 - R-6 + 6-Cl-rw

## THE DIY OF TATTING NECKLACE (14 / 15 STEPS)

### Step 14: make the bottom part of the modules

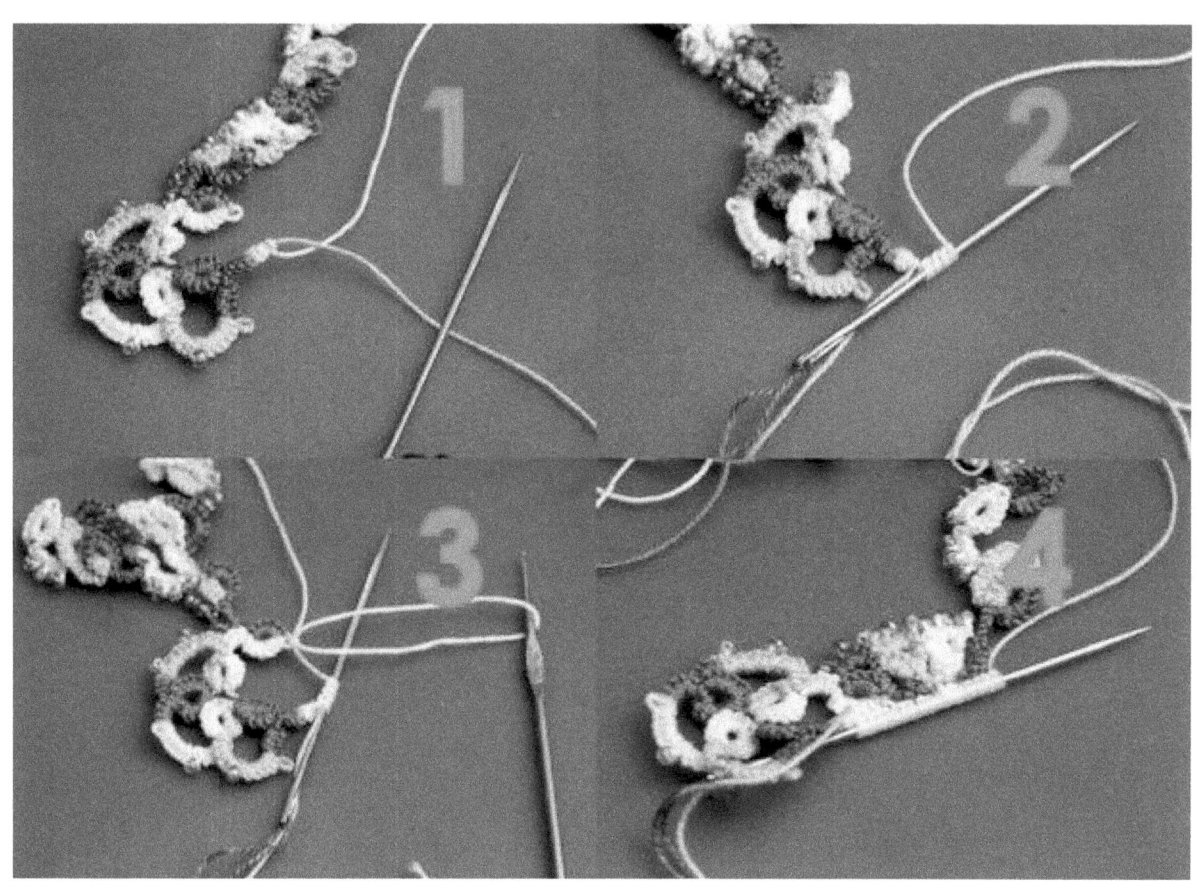

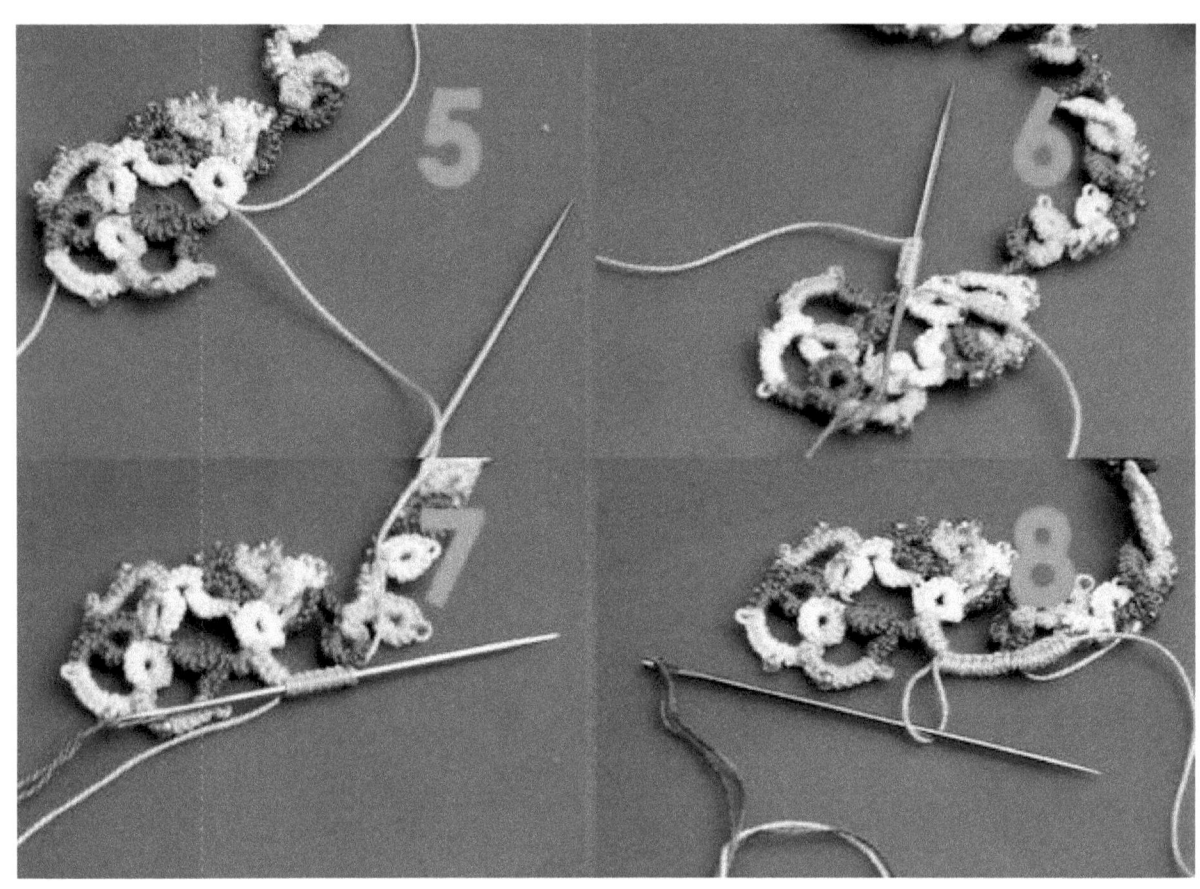

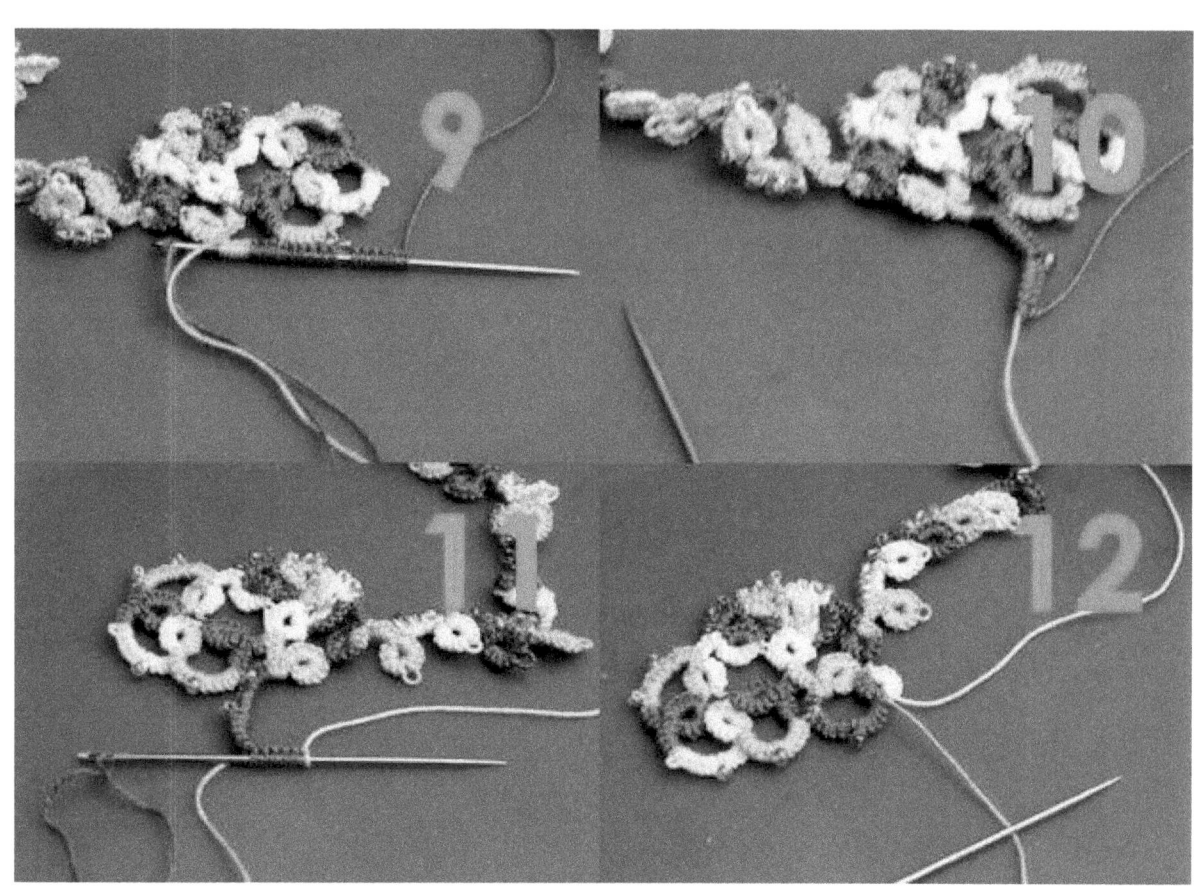

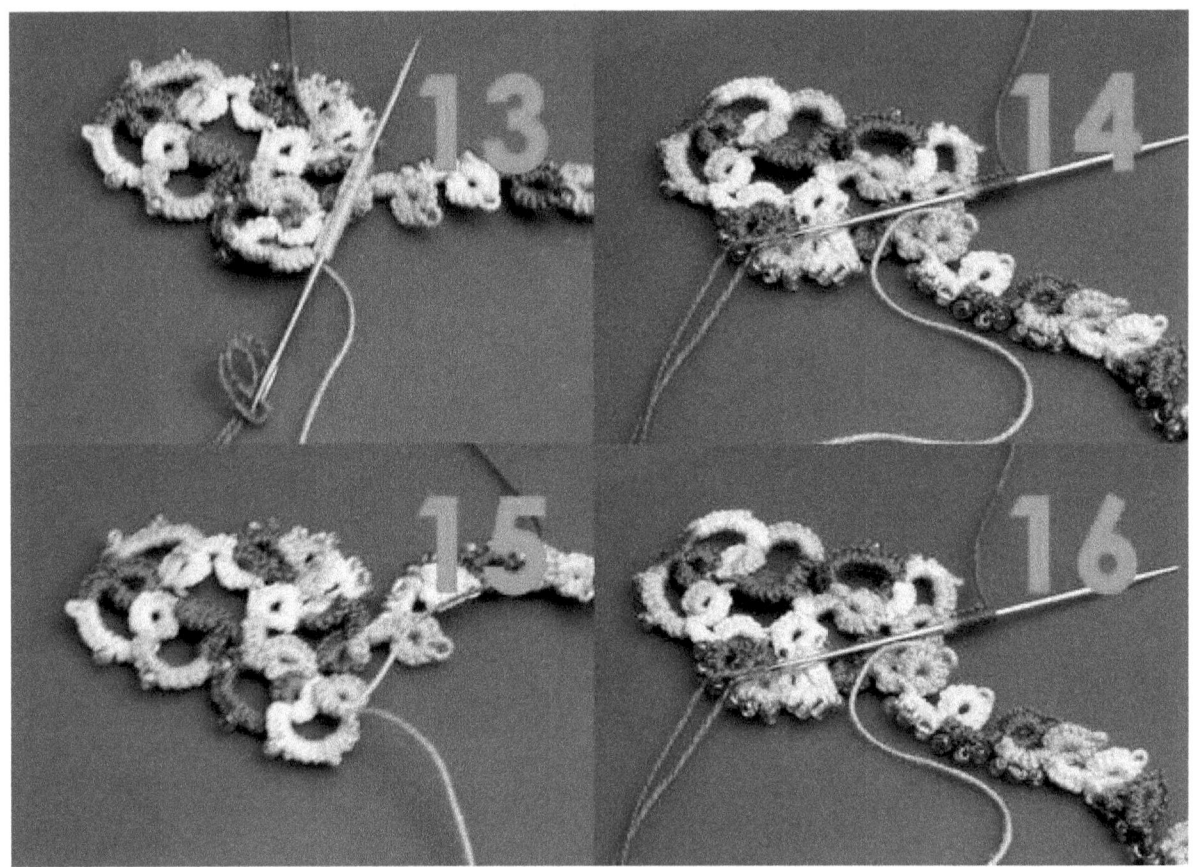

And finally, we have come to the beginning of the end of our work. The bottom of the modules.

This is by uniting the various rings on top, following the pattern established in the modules at both ends of the necklace.

We will continue the pattern:

30 - ch-6-yo-rw

31 - R-4 + 2 + 2 + 2 + 4-Cl-rw (here we make the large ring, connecting the 4 ring pins at the top of the module, closing at the end as d habit in the rings)

32 - ch-6-yo-rw

33 - R-6 + 6-Cl-rw (this ring must join the central ring is located between the modules)

34 - ch-6 + 6 b 6-yo-rw (this chain is linked to the Picot point in the chain of the previous module, to join the different modules of the collar)

35 - R-6 + 6-Cl-rw

36 - ch-6B6p6-yo-rw (point Picot of this chain is then join the lower part of the next module)

## THE DIY OF TATTING NECKLACE (15 / 15 STEPS)

Step 15: end of necklace

Repeat steps 30-36, which form the bottom of the module, as many times as necessary to end our necklace.

Finally, when you reach the top of the last module still to be reached, finish the job by joining the first module, which we created at the beginning of the pass.

At this time, in step 36, instead of making a Picot stitch, will join the yarn with the Picot stitch from the bottom of the initial collar of the module, so close to the bottom and therefore able to complete the module with the large ring inside.

We will continue the pattern:

36 (special end) -Ch-6 b 6 + 6-yo-rw

37 - R-6 + 6-Cl-rw

38 - ch-6-yo-rw

39 - R-4 + 2 + 2 + 2 + 4 -Cl-rw

40 - ch-6 + (join with initial ring) -yo

MAKE a SMAL knot and cut the thread!

Now we're just going to add the Collar Closures, Pimples Sewing Items left blank at both ends of the collar.

And good luck!

**THE END**

Milton Keynes UK
Ingram Content Group UK Ltd.
UKHW051445040424
440588UK00003B/42